Couldn't Prove, Had to Promise

Johns Hopkins: Poetry and Fiction

John Irwin, General Editor

Also by Wyatt Prunty

Couldn't Prove Had to Promise

Poems by Wyatt Prunty

Johns Hopkins University Press
Baltimore

This book has been brought to publication with the generous
assistance of the Albert Dowling Trust and the Writing Seminars
Publication Fund.

Johns Hopkins University Press
2715 North Charles Street
Baltimore, Maryland 21218-4363
www.press.jhu.edu

Library of Congress Cataloging-in-Publication Data

Prunty, Wyatt.
    [Poems. Selections]
    Couldn't prove, had to promise : poems / by Wyatt Prunty.
       pages; cm.—(Johns Hopkins: poetry and fiction)
    ISBN 978-1-4214-1714-1 (softcover : acid-free paper)—
    ISBN 1-4214-1714-6 (softcover : acid-free paper)—
    ISBN 978-1-4214-1715-8 (electronic)—ISBN 1-4214-1715-4 (electronic)
    I. Title.
    PS3566.R84A6 2015
    811'.54—dc23   2014035084

A catalog record for this book is available from the British Library.

*Special discounts are available for bulk purchases of this book. For
more information, please contact Special Sales at 410-516-6936 or
specialsales@press.jhu.edu.*

Johns Hopkins University Press uses environmentally friendly book
materials, including recycled text paper that is composed of at least 30
percent post-consumer waste, whenever possible.

For John and Meme

Contents

I

Making Frankenstein

He could not, *no*, he could not, *no*, although
He wheedled and cajoled, begged and promised,
But they would not, *no*, they would not
Take him to see *The Curse of Frankenstein*.
Then his uncle called and offered and they caved.
    So next it was the matinee then home
And nothing said, until he sat through dinner like
A little diplomat, and after that excused himself
And took his plate and headed up to bed.
Still nothing said. *No*, but midnight he woke screaming.
Morning, his father cleared the plates then turned,
"That's *that*," he summarized, "too anatomical."
"What's anatomical?" the boy asked back.

    This was summer 1957.
Monarchs foraged flowers, working colors
With their yes-now-no-now light arrhythmias.
By afternoon leaves shimmered in the heat,
And in the evening intermittent waves
Of fireflies telegraphed their kind
While in the little deeps of darkened houses
Window units swallowed oceans of air,
Until the boy, deep in his house, slept hard enough
That when he woke he couldn't close his hands.
"But what was anatomical?" he asked again.

    His father climbed a ladder to the attic where
He bumped around then climbed back down
Carrying an old foxed *Gray's Anatomy*

Packed full with illustrations, what seeing these
The boy felt certain were the pictures of mixed meats.
    That night the windows purred, and nothing budged,
Till breakfast brought another book, this time
One on pathology, which meant more pictures plus
Diseases, where the worst were best
And came from "intimate contact."

    "But what was intimate?" he later pestered,
Till his father downed his drink and said,
"That's how you made your way into this world."
Mother rose and left the room. The boy sat silent;
He sat there calmer than the noggin of a cat,
Until he stretched and, yawning, mentioned that
He might just go on up and get to bed.

    But secretly he understood; he knew
For good-and-always that in fact
His father wasn't a serious man
So he was on his own and had to make
Sense out of things himself, even if
Some sense went wrong, like Frankenstein's,
Who wasn't a serious man either—
And *that* was *really that*, even if it meant
You'd sink one day without so much as SOS.
    Some nights that summer, sleepless, eyes pinned wide,
He'd slip outdoors to watch his parents on the porch,
Their cigarettes, their quiet talk, and then,
For nothing he could tell, their laughter as
His father fixed another round of drinks.
And after that more laughter, like cicadas.

The boy watched this, as now he sometimes drives
The five miles out-of-way to see that house again.
And, never-you-mind his knowing better,
Sometimes just his doing this sets off
Imaginings that he is standing in the kitchen
Saying, "Oh my dear animal family,
How I loved you. How richly we purred."

And sometimes too it sweeps back over him,
His thinking that his father wasn't a serious man.
Those times, slowing the car, he says to himself,
"Well then, you are not a serious man either."

Rules

First day, first grade, two cut-ups laughing,
Shoving, shouting, till each called before
The teacher's desk. Knuckles rapped
And scolded back, the two act up again.

Things went like that, first-grade-first-day, until the girl
Who sat between the two had raised her hand
Announcing she was ill, which got her out
And down the hall and safely to the nurse.

Fourth time same day, the school nurse telephoned.
Then mother there, buckling her daughter,
So each of them, front-and-back,
Eyeing the other in the mirror,

Till the mother, slowing, said,
"You can't go to the nurse
Every time some bad thing happens."

And the mirror asked, "Where *do* you go?"

Thin

Declaring war on household order,
Grabbing the apples, oranges, anything,

Then racing out, we had our own ideas of order.
And Bill Burke's dad was dead, shaving in the mirror.

This was 1955;
Everyone else was still alive.

What would they have us children do back then?
We were very brave, and very thin.

When night came, deepening our windows,
We saw it like the lost eyes of dark mirrors.

Night came, and we were brave to sleep again.

Crescent Theater, Schenectady, NY

Thin silhouette below the screen,
The best part was the way he nodded yes
And kept up playing as the movie ran
More-or-less in time with itself.

That train converging on a washed-out bridge,
Or biplane spinning overhead,
Or Chaplin's cabin on the edge
Of so much gold or nothing—nothing said,

Only accompanied, and always by
Some melody struck up between
Disaster this side that side comedy,
With everything eliding scene-to-scene.

But now the camera's cranking so the land-
scape stutters while the biplane rights itself
And Harold Lloyd hangs from his minute hand
And Chaplin spins his cane and totters off.

And then there is that bridge which means the train's
Rerunning in a flashback therefore late
For what's already happened next. Sparks rain
Out of reversing wheels. The worst must wait,

As now the camera pans long distances,
Broad tinted fields, *The End*, old names…
To which that silhouette keeps nodding yes,
Yes to every last jittery frame.

Then house lights up and closing down,
He walks out with one melody
Stuck in his head. It circles round
So more refrain than melody, some sympathy

Captions won't explain. Whatever will?
The New World's arguments through neighborhoods
Where something goes on filling bill-
boards and windows? Or just what's understood

When home he reads his foreign paper's news,
Listening to his children using English
For everything they wish.
Rain falling somewhere else.

The Gladiator of Misgivings

The small boy with the booming voice,
Whose father seemed forever on a trip,
Knew what to do. We pushed the crates
Together, tumbled the cat-ruined carpet
Down the attic steps to the garage,
Then strung the Christmas lights and lettered signs
That shorted Shakespeare of his final *e*.

  After that, Lionel Higgenbotham took the stage,
Telling us he was Prince Hall and we,
We were those soldiers of the great events.
  Our audience was H's mother
Who would sometimes read from Tennyson,
Having us repeat each line; repeat again.
And there was also H's ancient aunt
Who smiled and nodded *yes* to everything.
  But once, out on the vasty fields of France,
Even the aunt had darkened thoughtfully
As looking back Hall said, "All right you Bustards, *Charge*."
  And with our brooms and garbage lids, we did.

Promise

Rain from a low November sky
That looks off-zinc or old aluminum,
Some steeped corrosive gray that ruins within
So every second equals something less.
The hall clock thumps the way an oar
Will work a lock or boat nudge at a pier
So boredom is a slow count through
Warped windows, trees like eelgrass,
Or a sky seen underwater where
Someone pulls hard while looking up,
Myopic as his need to breathe.

Outside, the world runs generalized.
Rain pools and wrinkles level-down-
to-level-down so stick-choked creeks
And blind ravines overtop their banks,
Take up their silts and sediments and leave.
Meanwhile the boy who watches this
Waits like a jon boat balancing,
Too flat to tip, too flat for hurrying.
Standing watch one window wide,
Rehearsing all he's heard before,
He tells himself, "You cross McNeely's river-woods
And slip the trees then wade the field,
Climb in the blind and wait the sun
Turning water to magnesium,
Tin-coated steel, pin-riddled plate,
And after that birds circling
And giving down gray into deeper gray."

But now out on the road an old car leans
So looks to be a tipping box slowing where
It turns, dips down, rattles the planked,
Percussive bridge, chews river gravel
Up the drive then cuts out hard across the yard
Where rocks itself down to a soft-sprung stop...
Consolidates, becomes the 1940 Oldsmobile
The old man says he will not quit
Because he bought it just before the War. And won.
The car stands idling. And the boy
Is out and down the steps before
His mother finishes his name.
It takes an entire body pulling
A 1940 door back closed.

"We'll get those ducks," the dry voice says,
"But first we've got to see you set,"
Says that and nothing more. Then turns the wheel
So they are back the way he came.
And everywhere is standing water;
Only the road above, that and one field,
A cow, two calves, one bale of hay.
"You need to go?" the old man asks,
Nodding sideways, laughing like a smoker breathing;
"Anywhere we stop's already wet."
The boy just shakes his head, studies water,
Studies the road. Then there's a metal bridge
That takes them up and takes them down
Over a river without banks
So all you see runs wide-as-long.
"You take them on the rise," the dry voice says.

"You watch them coming down—
        They need you wait them that—
Let them settle then discover.
        Their having that completes your part."

        But now the car is slowing, turning,
Heading up a drive so gravel's all an argument.
        And they are there, low wooden building
Mostly windows but so many painted
        Makes a greenhouse shaded.
Inside, slow ceiling fans and yellowed lights
        And tables in long rows so spilling colors
In a Piedmont of piled clothing.

        "All we need," the old man says
To no one in particular, "is proper sizes"
        —Meaning jackets, waders, boots, coats, gloves,
All manner of what's best against damp cold—
        Till someone's talking where they follow
Passing tables either side, then others standing,
        Laughing at how short the long johns are.
"Like socks," they say. But then real socks,
        So *these*, they say, "must be the mittens"
...until boots and shirts beneath clear windows
        Where the entire world is standing water,
For the boy still calculating
        How one sweep of wings rounds down,
Locks and flutters, cloth-like stalling, then settles.

        "And 'take them on the rise?' " he thinks,
"But rise to where? Everything I know is here."

13

Till now there is a coat for him,
And someone's holding waders, so
   Another joke, another laugh
Lasting to the counter where
   A ceiling fan's still easy as
The old car's wipers. "*Keep-you-dry,*"
   One voice advises. "*Good-luck-that,*"
Another follows. Then the long room talking
   Weathers, waters, seasons, and migrations.
One story starts, a second pitches in,
   Then others adding, each correcting,
Each supplying what it is comes next, next,
   Until the boy, years older now, decides
That, yes, things were the way those stories ran,

   Just couldn't prove so had to promise.

Bluefin

Lacking the bloodhound's rush
To find what's lost, this one
Moseys through a darkness
Deeper than affection practices.

Better it dive alone
Than we go down
Where pressure crushes,
Heart compresses
So enlarges
What's still missing.

Bad Dog

He was a bad dog, and he did not care.
When nature called he stood and lifted there.
He chewed socks, rugs, and shoes, the rungs of chairs.
Put on a leash, he locked his legs. He would not budge.
Asleep, he barked and chased what was not there.
Awake, he barked and chased what was not there.
When danger knocked he shrugged.

I see him still that way, facing the door,
Floppy and kind, wet nose against the glass
Or scratching over ears where going bald,
Then sniffing round to find just where he lifted earlier;
The which he did just once more when at last
Nature called and he followed.

Long Summers

What could you do? You couldn't run away.
Things wound up found, there where the landscape held
As much as scattered, old barns, slack gates,
And leaning sheds with sides soft as their mosses.

But sometimes change came of itself,
Roll gusts and sinking temperatures
While sashes dropped and lawn chairs waited.
Lightning mapped high boundaries,
And empty barrels rolled the rafters.
Suddenly one day turned to full season,
Though seasons never lasted long.
Soon light, then heat, windows rattled up;
Voices dried the air.

Small Facts

The first one in late June and in tall grass
So from a distance looked as though
Some animal was down, a fox or dog,
Too in the open for good news.
Then walking closer what I found
Was just a fawn, mindlessly asleep,
Curled on itself and warming in the sun,
The mother gone.

        First day a fawn
Survives without a scent for predators,
So this one slept the safer with the mother
Yards away, watching under low branches.
        And then last week there was another.
And now this morning twins, this time their mother
Cleaning them while I watched from the porch.
This sort of thing occurs most every year,
As though there runs a close but ragged lineage
Following itself season to season;
Or else it is a doe gives birth
Not to her fawn but to a place
Revisited year after year.

        And there are other regions to my theory,
The *whys* one wanders into when
Encountering a buck who snorts and runs
Yet on another day, same place,
A heavy doe will drop her head and paw;

And there's the tall one bumps the feeder with her nose,
Sticking out her impudent tongue for seed
And staring through the window when the feeder's empty.

Then the world of rutting comes around,
After which we have to rake, and prop the fences;
Other months the bagatelles through early vegetation,
As though we served a salad every year
And only ought to add some vinaigrette.

But this day, watching one more dumb show of
Brief urgency and birth, the mother
Washing down and bedding down her two
Till they were near invisible among dead leaves,
All was as unremarkable as ever,
Indifferent, really, if still vulnerable.
"All just a little too routine," I said,
To nothing near enough to hear.

And then the mother wasn't there.
So I walked out to get a closer look.
And what I saw, spotted and wet
And not about to move, stared me back
Uncomprehendingly, eyes with
The clarity and vacancy
Of just-cleaned windows or an emptied glass.
They gazed out with a blank intensity
That seemed impossible to anything
That soon would hunger, leave and grow,
Survive and suffer, possibly return.

Beginning the Ending

The Pacific sun took lives to set.

This is early color, plus the speed is off.
The parents are slow. They've done all this before.
And now the wedding guests file through the door.
Their hats are funny, but no one laughs.

Then we are inside looking over rows
Of backs of heads agreed on what comes next,
Another short parade into old text
With two repeating what a third one says.

How can the young keep doing this?
How can they promise what they have no way of knowing,
All the improbable happiness
Of going where they cannot know they're going?

Tomorrow is unrented rooms;
Vows give no proof, and making them can lead to loss.
But never-you-mind, the little Bell & Howell hums;
Reality repays at cost.

And I see one who bent to light a smoke
And wore straw hats and carried a cane
And asked a question used a story to explain;
How wishing the War away he'd make a joke

And out-laugh everyone; then pause, inhale.
Such times the future seemed suspended,
Like new orders in the mail
Or long deployments not yet ended.

Endings came of course, like this one,
People bunched and smiling, waving.
Or no; those people frozen, something broken,
Half-frame edging where it's gnawing

In the light above a sprocket stuck
With all that just won't happen.
But then smiles again, hands wave; cars start, drive out.
The film plays out, feathering the white plane

Of an old screen hung as though bleached tapestry
Contained the War's entire expanse
Past ending—when the bride will be
A bride again, smiling a different tense

With what she calls "late happiness,"
As heat waves ripple sunlight out of blacktop
Where one road runs on, as hope must run, since
Starting argues some place is the one place you will stop.

What Kind

Personalize it, if you must. Somewhere
Love's gone off for a weekend in the mountains
Or to the beach; love's driving somewhere other
Than your little life, watchful and welcoming fan
Of yourself, to what was always coming anyway—
Something like expensive fixtures hanging from
High ceilings with a light so generalized
You are your old self even as you're not,
Reiterative to the end, not scared exactly,
Just slowing as you feel someone familiar
Taking your side in things, cooling you down
On things, and by that making you
Think of tomorrow more fondly than before.

Checks & Balances

Lion paced his cage then stood and roared
Till monkey screamed and climbed a tree,
As though by this the two agreed
That lion was carnivore
And terror on the other side
Was what Zoo fed him for.

But monkey had a trick he'd learned.
When smokers passed he danced a fit
With begging through the bars till one returned
And handed him a cigarette,
Which he then puffed and studied as it burned,
Then flicked the butt just where the lion turned.

Another Christmas Tie This Year

That is green and red and longer than usual
And worn by you over another Christmas dinner
Where you are smiling down the table and taking stock.
You're sixty-five; you've got your health.
You've got your job; you like to work.
Left and right, your smiling kids are out of school.
They've got their health, their jobs, their plans.
They say they like to work. They save.
And tonight they are laughing with tears in their eyes.

Far end, there is your wife, laughing.
She is beautiful in ways Jane Fonda never figured out.
And so much younger too, such that the both of you
Know who, time comes, will do the tucking in.
—And she will live on well, because she is,
Well, she is younger than you,
And so kind about the things she cannot change,
Like you. Not that you're not distinguished in
Your quiet world, where you are far too modest
Ever to wear that rack of medals you deserve
But live instead as though some gray Olympian
Who likes to give the second place a second chance....

And you are Chamberlain and Russell and Bird,
And Roland Kirk, Monk, Brubeck, and the other Bird,
And Melville and Hardy enjoying a good laugh on a sunny day.
You are the hidden redwood in your side-yard's undergrowth
Bordering a cul-de-sac of grave reflection

Where your neighbors never park their cars quite right.
And you do not mind that always
You must look down a bit to see these things.
No, really, the only worry about your looking down just now
Might be to find some small spot of something on your brand new tie.

       Until in order to say grace, hands rising to your lap, you *do* look
          down,
Bowing your head while a grave moment stretches through your family's
       silence.
       You look down and see in fact there is no spot on your tie,
No spot at all, because while sitting down
You let the tie sink into the gravy boat, where it has settled
And lost the long flat bough of holly with red berries it was meant to
       represent.
       There it is, stilled and changed above your washed and separate
          hands...
Which now you join, saying grace anyway;
And meaning it a little more than would have
Been the case with only a *small* spot on your tie.

Reading the Map

Whatever bearing you select,
Eventually your path will intersect
Such variance in elevation you will find you need
A topographic map for where things lead.

Brunton Pocket Transit opened,
Orient yourself so compass rose, legend, and
Coordinates confirm the route
You've picked. That done, pack up, set out,

Following the arguments of contour lines,
From rock and rise to water and decline
To where, in order it be accurate,
Cartography exaggerates.

By scale, that bridge your map identifies
Should be invisible, but there it lies,
As bold in print and pixel-wide
As the hurried river it divides,

Past which the landscape's slow relief
Devolves with roll and slip beneath
Every step you take, following a trail
That, in order to be read, is inaccurate to scale,

As map and compass make one motion
Out of strike, dip, fault, contact, and foliation,
Weaving and woven where, roads and bridges
Are the duplicates of valleys, ridges,

Every aspect arguing some other,
As love intends and maps assume: two put together,
Even when just one is represented—
This road, that bridge, or *you*, could you be printed,

Clearly standing out of scale, yet there you are—
Ready for imagination's little car
Driving a world that turns into
Whatever conformations you pass through,

A landscape written upper case
And in bold print, like memory, and traced
Even where there are no pixels,
Even as, reading the map, love is invisible.

ad lib

Just told he had six months, he said,
"A fat old sedentary diabetic
Such as me? I could have caught a heart attack
Last Saturday and now six months get added?"

Visits ended with his laughing
At the finches circled round his feeder,
Groundling squirrels elbowing under,
And crows who proved unable to stop scolding.

Something silent went on eyeing
While the sun confirmed one angle, then another,
And trees collected in the shade they gave each other.
And once, as we were leaving,

He called after, "I enjoy seeing you
So much sometimes I forget I'm dying.
No, that's not it. What I mean is sometimes
There's some part of me *stops* dying."

Nod

When in the middle of the afternoon
On a well-marked asphalt parking lot
I came to myself standing among the SUVs
Where the yellow lines and exit signs were lost,
And where the July heat was oil and wave
Altering the eye of everything
So overhead the sun looked oxidized
While underneath, moments of silica winked
Out of a field of black mica,
        Right then, turning about, seeing
So many little lights blinking up from black,
I stopped and said, "Fulton, Fulton,
Just look at it would ya, the gloves are off,
But that just means they're scattered on the mat.
The entire world has parked and packed it in.
Any old fight's better having than having this.
This is the flu before the fever touches you,
The ache without a place to point,
Shadows hiding the end of the alley
And an entire block of locked back doors;
This is the neighborhood of calls
For children and dogs who never return,
That little land where sleep lies down
And no one thinks to wake her up.
        Bring me back the pounding shoe and the gray Navy
Flushing Russian submarines. Give me that stretch
Where longing lives—space shots and Aaron up to bat,
Black coffee and the small collaterals

Of penny postcards, pets, T-Bills meaning what they say.
Steady the hall clock's scissoring hands
So shirts are buttoned up and down at once
And smiles stay fixed at flashbulb best.
Give me, in short, a new deck, a fresh cut,
Another deal, a winning hand,
As that's what needs some bringing back."

    But of course there was no Fulton,
As over time the cars all idled off,
Till I studied the mercury vapor lights,
Counted the empty parking spots
Then, addressing Fulton anyways,
Who's always somewheres else about,
And me speaking a little too bravely too,
Just talking a little too much through my summer hat,
Said to Fulton, said to me,
                "So it begins, my rambling boy."
    And saying that, I heard a laugh
That was a wheeze that was a cough,
As looking round I saw a coal go bright, go dark,
Redden then fade, redden again, then disappear—
Some smoker working backwards from his light,
Thumb-to-finger, elbow out, till arm thrown forward
Weakly as exaggerated Nixon,
He dropped his hand, exhaled and coughed again,
Then cleared his throat and pointed with his cigarette:

    "That lot ain't clover is it, Bud;
What d'ya think you're looking for?"
    "Not a thing," I said.

"Thing?" a little breath of smoke spoke back.
"Now that's a category, ain't it, Bud.
And a fibber of an argument as well,
Much like that friend you say you got, what's his name?
Fuller, Flap? That guy's about as real
As Mrs. Thatcher sleeping in the back seat
Of a Mercury, some choir singing her
The hymn of human happiness and misery."

Stepping from the door, he stood so's I could see.
He had big teeth that made him look to smile.
But he didn't smile. Wire glasses, sunken chest,
Thin tie and gray fedora cocked and caved,
He stared ahead but had the backward eyes
Of someone saying A while thinking B.
Nodding, he said, "Wife will tell ya"
(a tall woman was struggling from
the backseat of an old low Mercury,
a thin boy seated crookedly behind the wheel),
"Wife will tell ya everything you'll ever sing, friend;
Then how it is you will forget the words
So make some up and whistle round
Till you have fumbled back to where you started out.
But look you now, you out of cash, bump your noggin?
Forget your number? Need a lift?
That's me. I'm in security. I make the calls:
I know what holds—fire doors and double locks.
There's nothing like a blaze one side
And on the other, the breathable air of reliable escape.
So step this way; use any name you like,
Just look about and net you up a list of wants.

The shops are thinning out so now there's room
To see what gives you appetite."
          Next, he was battling a double door,
Till shouldering inside he said,
"I know this stretch the way I know
That modesty shoplifters use
When touching things they mean to take,
Clothes under signs announcing sales,
Or items on less prominent displays—
Same as I know that shopper's ways
Beside the fitting room where going in
All baggy clothes, she marches back
Fleshed out with ten pounds off the rack.
I know the stolen cards, the stiff-kneed walk
From store to store, some idiot kid
Thinking to beat the call that trips the lights,
And I know that kind of idleness that hesitates
Then lifts and makes a comic break.
That is my business, knowing the want that waits
Like sly forgetfulness, caged innocence.
          But never you mind my talking shop—*shops*, I mean—
They're always better when the folks are out.
So just you look about. I have a call to make."
          And so what next? And so I walked,
Passing one store then another.
But who is it ever starts one way
And doesn't wind up turning someway other?
First leg shifts, the second gets the weight
And off you go, this-way-then-that.

And that is just the way I made my way,
As on my left there was a store
With compasses—no maps; and lamps—no books;
And carpets but no furniture...
And next to these, a window full of clocks
Announcing different times, and under those
Recliners like exhausted yawns.
        While on my right there were bookstores
And cooking stores, wine shops and shops for shoes and hats,
Then outing gear, more shoes, more hats,
Gimmick bathroom scales and telephones,
Bird baths, bird feeders, wall thermometers,
Fake antique radios, air purifiers,
A pet store where two Scotties barked,
And either side of these two slow aquariums
Where color swam through color,
While overhead an ornate cage
Held the day's bright birds folded for the night.
        Through all this, under and among all this,
A girl was stepping cage to cage,
Until she stopped, looked up and waved,
Then dropped her arm and turned away.
        And in the time she took to turn
That wheeze, that cough was back, tapping a smoke
Until he thumbed a match and without looking
Brought it up: "Who's to remember," he said,
"Who's to remember, a nickel or a dime
Or ever the time you saw your little dog get hit?"
        "And how you think you know my dog was hit," I said.
"I'm saying, you were six; the dog was four,
Maybe five. Just saying that, nothing more.

No, but it rolled, didn't it? Stood, then rolled,
Looked, searching you to breathe. And what I think
You thought that animal was thinking then
Was what I like to call that lethal lack of hope
Seen in tired motels, slumped waiting rooms,
Discarded magazines, cuff links and watches with
Initials no one now knows how to read."
        He stalled on that, studied his shoes.
Then started again. "Children and pets!"
He said, studying some mid-air vacancy.
"Those and the pleasure of mockingbirds
And attic fans running on all night. But too,
Plagues and wars, bank runs and losing seasons,
Brilliant crashes, knuckled wrecks—sometimes I hear
The entire chorus in the white noise of
My central air." He stopped again,
Dropped his smoke, looked down, toed it flat,
Then nodded toward a mannequin—
Blue blazer, bucks and yachting cap, sanded face.
        "Some guy wants to tell me how a heart gets full,
Give reason why a soldier can't go home,
The world too big to fit his rearview mirror,
Some such? I say, don't waste your needle
On that thread. It never knots; and the wool won't hold.
Besides, you bundle up because it's cold,
You're only living in the cold."
        "It's July 3," I said. "We're standing in a mall
Outside Atlanta, Georgia. It's nearly dark,
And no one's thinking anything but heat.
Just ask your wife out in that parking lot,
Stuck with that cashed-in car you've got."

"*Settle, settle*," he said, palms to my face.
"You're right about the car, cashed in for sure,
And running rough. And wife out there...
Well now, just ask her what a word like *rough* might mean.
      But to our situation here, these stores—
You hold a map and phonebook side-by-side,
You're any place you please. They're all the same:
Miami to Chicago as Boston to L.A.
You got your size, they got your fit."
      After that, he lifted his hat,
Looked over his glasses, eyebrows up,
Then let the hat drop back and said,
"All the news I have to tell you is
I've been to sea, steamed through the hurricanes,
Survived a wreck and floated the salt wave for three days,
Shoveled a forest fire, sand-bagged a flood,
Delivered my daughter on the kitchen floor
While the doctor talked me through by telephone,
Watched a twister swallow my house,
Lived on either coast and parts between,
And these and more leave me to tell you for
A certain fact that of all the places that I've ever been,
Well...this is one of them."
      Then he was searching his pockets
And taking his time too, till looking round
And speaking almost shyly, he said,
"You know, my honest name is Byrom Thatch,
But no one's ever called me anything but Floyd."

[2]
　　　"All right. All right" I said, "So Mr. Thatch,
So Mr. Floyd, and now the two of you
Staring from under the same fedora?
We're talking early blooms in sunlight where
A building's wall will block the wind
And let today pretend it is tomorrow.
We're talking why the front door opens from the back
As why the *whatnot* ends with *not*
When *get* comes second in *forget*.
　　　We're saying, *Reflect you now upon*
The deepening silence found in a sea of trouble,
And by that mean, *Sometimes there's more,*
But then again sometimes there's less,
Just like you better watch those mice
Who growing fat suggest the rats are gone,
As promise always begs another slice…
Which is to say, Floyd—standing here
You're better off than Byrom there."
　　　I nodded off to where a tall shape leaned,
Filling the pet store's sidewalk window.
It sidled, stopped, looked in, shifted, looked again,
Hands shading eyes and arms against the glass,
Then it was moving fast and headed for the double doors.

　　　"So-Byrom-So-Floyd," I said, picking it up,
"There's one thing more you might allow:
If all you've ever heard is Floyd instead of Thatch,
Or Byrom-Thatch, or, say, Floyd-Byrom-Thatch—
Well-then, that may just be the thing you bet
Your breakfast you will hear most anywhere…

As the finch will chatter in one light
But the swallow winks you from another.

It therefore seems right and fitting,
Or it fits about right, or, *It is right-*
about-like-this it fits to say
That all those hurricanes and twisters,
Those floods and wrecks and salt waves you report?
They're more like hyphens than what happened."

"*Hey—Hey!*" he said, eyes narrowing
Like Stilwell staring the bastards down,
"You don't have socks without some feet,
No hat but got some noggin.
I'm everything I said I was,
And truth remains, there was in fact
That cyclops of a hurricane."
Then nodding up-and-down and side-to-side
As though confirming *yes* and *no* at once,
Floyd said, "I meant things like the Gooney Bird
And how we thought up Burma-Shave.
I meant so many things, and most of them
Like laughter on long porches in warm weather,
Or the rhythms of a railcar swaying
Under a full moon flooding fields,
Or an old man snoring the deep-down-hall
Where the good dog curls with stopping the door.
I meant the way we say *egads, good grief, gadzooks,*
Or *Yo, Vinny, get a load of that stuff passing wouldya.*
I meant superlatives the way we do
When starching uniforms or raising flags,
Getting erections or stiff nipples.

Plus too, there is contentment to be praised,
As at day's end the sun will set
So every little pond of self
Deepens upward into night the way
A pet's dark eyes will watch a hand with food."

But then Floyd's voice had jumped a scale
As he was saying, "June, dear June, oh June,"
And all this in a tone of innocence
One takes for children's birthday parties
Or when driving them to get a shot
Or any place where parents will pretend
All the world's a beagle by the ears.
"We're here admiring animals," Floyd said,
Mouth like a cut, eyes siphoning.

"*Admiring*," June repeated, hands to waist,
Chin up and elbows out, feet wide.
"I am the bride," she said, turning my way
But never looking quite my way,
"I am the bride of all the little lies one hears—
From tickets fixed to false names signed
On hotel registries, from checks that bounce
To bouncing mattresses...such things as these,
Which burn in memory like low-watt bulbs
On summer porches where small flies will swarm,
Whispering themselves out of existence."
Then, still turned my way but gazing so
Her eyes were locked above my head, she added,
"I will tell you a secret, Little Mister—
Call for robin-redbreast or the wren,
Neither of these will hover again.

Only the absent hours fly.
Call either robin or the wren,
But neither will hover again."

And hearing that I could have been
Back down the hall investigating exit signs
Or searching storefront windows filled
With small collectibles. Floyd-Byrom-Thatch
Stood some feet off where striking a match
He cupped his hands, tilted his head,
Inhaled and held, exhaled, then dropping the match
Studied his hands—one palm up and one palm down.
        And just like that it settled over me
That though I was the one addressed
I also was the one excused from what was coming next.

        "I'll tell you, Little Mister," June said again,
"Whether you will or no, you know,
God loves his people much the way
His people love their pets, so there is this for you—
Something that-one-there has never understood."
She cut her eyes where Floyd looked down,
Still studying the separate practice of his hands.
"I took a tomcat once," June said,
"A feral, and I named him Foots
Because he had so many toes. Plus too,
He had his wander ways, such that
Come dinner, neighbors called to say,
'June, June, we have the cutest kittens needing homes,'
And I'd reply, 'How sweet, but I have Foots, you know.'
'We do know, June,' the other end would say;
'These kittens all have extra toes.'

Well, comedies like that will make
One laugh only so long. In time, I gave commands.
Not sleep, mind you, but an alteration
Of a kind I've come to recommend more days than not,
A method neither this one here
(She ran her eyes Floyd's way again)
Nor that cat then would ever comprehend."

Somewhere along the hall a hinge complained
And latch clicked shut, but by then June had turned
And frowning down on Floyd was saying,
"Oh my poor repeated error,
When will you ever understand
That Junie winds up seeing everything.
That's how her stories always end."

There was that hinge again,
Crying in a long note till a door thumped shut.
And this time hearing that, June cut things short.
Standing taller than before,
Eyes scouring the hall, she stilled
Like a big cat watching food.

And I stilled too, focusing great distances,
Like someone seated in reverse
Who sees the landscape run ahead and back at once—
As June kept staring over Floyd's fedora
And Floyd stood looking down as though
He read the future in his feet.

Then I was outside in that parking lot,
Which darker now seemed larger than before,
Its lights in yellow circles on the asphalt where
They made a kind of archipelago
By which there was nowhere to go.

And just like that my smoke, my cough was back
And standing near and asking me,
"Ever hear of the Answer Man?"
This in the slow pleuritic wheeze
Of someone drawing oxygen, that or
A Schrader valve letting your tire go flat.
        "*Answer Man,*" he said again, "hear of him?
He's in those stories from that war in which
The leaves are close as air so sound is sight
And standing watch becomes your life.
        Meanwhile, back in America
It's anti-war and Mardi Gras—
High numbers, sandals, beads, and silly smoke.
But in the East we had this little fact,
And I was mailed a ticket that.
        And when I made it home again—
I only had three friends, my Mom, my Dad, my dog.
And then I took my second tour, so when
I got back next I just had two. My dog had died."
        "But you," I said, "you're standing back inside."
        "And too," he answered, "here I am with you."
Then lifting his hat he squinted me good
And looked to smile. But he never smiled.

Out in the lot a car door slammed,
A starter whined and fan belt squealed
Until an engine caught and the old low Mercury
Came idling, all windows down,
The boy still seated crookedly
And staring through the steering wheel,
While in the shadow of the car's rear seat
Something twisted. Settled back.

[3]
The bootleg and the buttonhook,
The split-wide end for getting in
And then the chandelle and the Immelmann
For getting your bacon out again?
All these about as certain as
A miner's inch—now that the entire lot
Stood empty as a stadium in which
Both teams just lost.
But turning round, just looking back,
I saw a well-lit window framing
Tables, shelves, and racks, another mannequin,
And farther back, high over these,
Suspended by a line too thin to see,
There was a mobile of small paper birds
Oaring one way underneath a ceiling fan
That overhead clocked opposite.

Only what agrees can disagree like that—
Loud ties and madras coats, plaid shorts, pink shirts,
Wingtips and argyle socks, lawn parties where
The conversation climbs a cumuli
Of slow balloons, and never the smaller to the eye.

Indoors it's manufacture fills;
Outside the laughter's almost melody.
        Inside a second hand runs idiot
Or calendar will turn you out of date,
But through an opened window or
A door left wide the weather climbs
Its little tugs forever.

        Then just my thinking that, my friend,
My cough was back and talking fast—
"Games and races, wins and losses," he said,
"Things you can't explain until they're done
And-even-then you lack reliables.
        They're like your hyphens, Bud, but worse—
Abandoned buildings, gutted houses,
Visits paid you every time you're driving by
And something catches in your eye,
Some vacant window staring back
Till what it's not is what you've got.
        Or say you have a tire goes flat,
Or shifter seizes in a turn, or say
You hit a patch of ice, go withershins
So fill a ditch and sit there staring
What-to-when till someone stops and lends a hand.
        There is a hyphenate in that;
A gap between your life and where
You thought your life was going.
        Or say I *am* more hyphens than what happened.
If so, that's why I'm in security;
I don't believe in no one's side.
I only stock in doors that lock."

Thatch nodded in agreement with himself
Then pointed where the pet store clerk
Was walking out with something in her arms.
It twisted round, she tightened up,
Looked left-and-right, then stepped into
The headlights of a waiting car.
Once on the other side, she handed in
What she was holding, then she folded after.
The car eased up, June at the wheel,
The crooked boy sitting in the back,
Smiling over what the clerk had brought.
"And what is this?" I thought out loud.
"And what is this?" Floyd mimicked back.
"You mean what water carries salt like that?
It's everything I said it was;
It's games and races you can't know
Since while they're running no one says
Which bets are wins and which ones losses."

The Mercury was rolling now,
Two headlights like skimmed milk across
The asphalt where they spilled ahead
Through pale recurrent edges.
Floyd watched until the car was gone
Then cut a look my way, turned halfway round.

"Since we're still here," he said, "I mine-as-well
Point out one fact for certainty:
Your Fulton isn't anything you hope;
He's like an egg without a yolk,
A thread without a knot."

"Oh Fulton's just a family term," I said,
"A way of saying things gone opposite."

"You mean your Fulton is a lie?" Floyd asked,
Staring hard, eyes brighter than before.
"A lie can tell you someone closer than
The truth will do. A lie has motive,
Uses reason, has real opposites,
And those are things we understand.
A lie has cause and that's a probable;
A lie's reliable."

"Fulton's just for emphasis," I said.
"So *now*," Floyd slowed, "you're telling me
Fulton is the word you use for swearing?
Swearing makes a match for lying, only better,
Like politicians taking office,
Courtrooms and car dealerships,
Old meat, red dye, all labels changed.
Swearing makes a probable reliable as lies.
And then there is the body and its sex;
Those two are good for swearing.
And names and pieties, they work as well.
Swear words and lies, fire doors and locks,
They separate and make a sense
Never a thirst got quenched."
"I never meant what you just said," I said.
"It doesn't matter *how* you meant it, Bud.
The words are words; they wait you out.
Meanwhile, your swearing makes one fine beginning."

"You sure do know a lot," I said, "for someone
Who just opens up then closes down again."
Floyd contemplated my small meanness
Till his face relaxed into a smile.
Studying his palms, he said,
"Meybe so; just meybe so.
It's closing always means the most;
That's how the joke will work you best.
It makes you feel you're getting more by giving less."
Then Floyd looked where the Mercury
Had turned and disappeared.
"Policies and prices," he said, "it's always words
And never a one to stanch a wound
Or fetch a body back. So what's it more
To do than open up and lock back down?
You got your name sewn in your coat
Because you're losing it; you're on a train
And looking back, arm raised to wave,
But doing that your hand just opens empty—
Says goodbye one side, and all it is you lack the other.
You tell me Fulton's just a saying,
Just another Mrs. Calabash?
I tell you he's a swear, that's all.
There's totals, Bud; there's swears and totals,
One to open, one to shut you down again,
And any mouth says otherwise
Ain't got the spit to hock a quid.

You take the Answer Man. Now *he* was totals.
He knew before he asked. And God he was
A patience. You hurt so bad you couldn't say,

Well he could wait you out. He never was a one
That wouldn't finish. He always give it time.
He was a cold fact in that manner."

"If I were you there Floyd," I said,
"Or Mr. Thatch or else Floyd-Byrom-Thatch,
I'd make me up a brakeman song
And lift my hat and wave that idea off."
"Meybe you would," Floyd said, eyeing me.
"But what I got, you got as well.
You're like that blue-tail fly caught in a window,
Trapped and speeding up because the light is heating up."

"That notion's yours," I said, "no kind of mine."
"*Liar*," he said, squinting me good,
Tightening a penciled mouth.
"You're sworn like me, just younger's all.

Go make you up a story like
A Christmas tree, or maybe like
An old hall tree stacked full of coats
And people in some other room
And all of them returning soon.
Just make you up a story of what's not,
Much like this empty parking lot.
Do that and see who's it returning."

"All right," I said. "All right, I will."

[4]

It's-July-1953-
and-dark-outside-and-every-room-indoors-
is-hot, so now the boy walks out to where
The moon's a silver plate suspended
Over fields, hedgerows, a barn with gambrel roof
And sideways these, exaggerated shadows
Through the landscape's cows and goats, one bull, two mules,
The blind horse by the gate, and in a tree
A mockingbird who summarizes all.
      The boy heads where his father laughs.
His uncle has said something funny.
They're talking "gin and cotton." They sound certain.
They drink the gin, discuss the cotton.
      Then as the boy steps close
The uncle's voice climbs up a bit,
As now he's all about a milk cow
Lives on onions, and a mule that likes
To change its mind. And then there is
The goat that takes the stairs up to
The loft to have his slash of hay
And eats so much he winds up lost
Inside the bales until one day
He's chewed him free the entire way
Back out the other side.
      And next there is the horse that flies
While underground an old potato eyes
The soles of those who walk him overhead—.

      Some of this the boy has heard before.
He knows the horse that flies is from a book,
And knows the rest is like a joke…

The way his sister says his ears
Are like an elephant's but larger,
And that he has an inconvenient memory.
        She likes to say he's like a thing
You get for free but didn't want,
And even if he did know how to write
Santa wouldn't read his letter.
She says it's hard to be so nice
When everything before was better.
She tells him that his head is full of feathers.
        The father and the uncle talk;
The bird presides encyclopedically.
        Then for some reason both men laugh.
Then both turn serious. It's what
They call "entailment." That is the subject now,
Until the uncle says, "The cotton goes to gin,"
And they both laugh again.
                            Their glasses sweat.
        And the boy can't answer what that means,
Much as he wonders why
You write your numbers so they add
But then you spell them so they don't.

        Studying such, just gazing up,
Not thinking anything particular,
He sees what looks to be the horse that flies
Except it only rises, climbs the higher
In one place and never the smaller where it goes.
        "See that," the boy says to himself.
"See *that*," he says again, louder,
Tugging his father's arm to point.

But the father's busy talking. Talking.
Not until the boy looks down is there
A way to make him listen.
　　　　"*See*," the boy repeats, pointing where he means.
But when he looks again there's nothing there.

　　　　"It climbed but never got the smaller," he says.
　　　　"It must have been an owl," his father answers.
　　　　"Or else the Phantom after you," the sister adds.
　　　　"It was an owl," the father says a second time,
"So low it caught the angle of your eye.
That low and fast, an owl can look like anything."
　　　　"Like the Phantom," the sister says,
"Because you rival him in ugliness
So he is jealous, and he's here
To get you when you fall asleep."

And when the boy explains again,
The father says, "An angel? *No*.
I said an *angle*, an angle from your eye,
Which means you saw an owl is all,
Flying low and hurrying."
　　　　"For what?" the boy asks absently.
　　　　"You saw it from the corner of your eye,"
The father tells him patiently.
　　　　"That made it look the farther off,
But it was overhead; that's why
You saw it differently."
　　　　"Phantom's different," sister says;
　　　　"Or else it was a bat come close," the uncle adds.

But-never-you-mind-what-they-will-say
As now the boy is upstairs in his bed
Watching his little movie run itself
Start-to-finish. It always ends in silver,
Then starts again, and he keeps watching,
Proving that he's not afraid, just waiting for
The others when they take the stairs to bed.

"And right there Floyd," I summed it up,
"You have yourself a story of what's not
That settles on what is."

Floyd's eyes were off and on their own,
As they continued gazing all the distance
It now took for him to telescope
From boredom back to irritation.
          "That's a catch you'll never eat," he said.
"We quit that kind of net four wars ago;
Had to quit or else we'd lose.
But just to lend a little balance, Bud,
I'll tell you for the recollection
It's my daddy was the farmer
Yours and your uncle never made.
          My daddy had his cotton too,
Plus animals. And he could hunt.
He made things grow, but then he knew
To cut 'em down again.
          I seen him take three shots and drop five quail;
And once a turkey flushed straight up,
He dish-ragged that so never needed cleaning.
          I seen him dust the backsides off two mules
And kill a neighbor's dog just for barking.

And goats and cows, he bled 'em out
And squared 'em up and ate 'em without comment.
I seen my daddy pull a dead calf out a cow
And butcher it before the steam was off.
You're hungry, you will welcome that."

"And where'd your daddy live?" I asked.
"That's never been a certainty of fact," Floyd said,
Cutting his eyes an angle off.
"For all he did outside he lived indoors.
But sparrows and minnows, mosquitoes and fleas,
He knew the list of it right down to those."

"You talk him such," I said,
"Just where's his fixed address these days?"
"A lifetime's not the answer that," Floyd said.
Eyes grazing over the parking slots,
All of them empty.

"My daddy threw me out and down
So here I am with you, and that's the all of it.
But I should add, before my daddy put me
On the road I had my reasons leaving too,
Like when I met those orange-tailed wasps
Furious of a summer's afternoon.
It's hard to flush them, then you do,
God you're a stumble and a sorry.
My daddy let me walk unknowing into that.
Then did he ever hear me howl. But he just watched.
Now why'd he let a thing like that get on my back?
He, who always knew the next-and-next of it;
You tell me why he let his own like that."

"I can't," I said.

"You bet you can't...

And why you think he threw me out?"

"Don't know," I said.

"That's right; don't know.

It was I mimed him good, that's why.

He caught me doing that and threw me down

Where now there is no getting back

And all of that for funning him.

But *could* I make the others laugh!

Had to be he hated that 'cause with a twitch

He threw me out and down to where

I landed hard and got stoved-up

So now I have a sunken chest and nervous eyes

And never sleep for what it's coming next—.

That's why I work security.

But all I ever meant was be like him.

I drive myself around exactly how he did.

He always said I did, just sometimes in reverse;

He said I was original in that

Such that no one come close to me.

So why'd he stove my ribs like that,

Or let that orange-tailed coven after me?"

"You tell *me* why," I said; "my patent's out."

"Nobody," Floyd said tightly back, "ever owns a patent."

His pupils were black mica.

"It's all of it," he said, "indifferent manufacture.

But I *was* like my daddy. And I imitated him.

What more a father want? You always imitate

What you believe.

One night I get
A little drunk and mimic him
The way he opened animals
And *slam* he sails me down where there's
No chance for ever climbing back.
        But I was just in compliment to what he meant.
And like I said, we imitate what we believe.
Meanwhile, he sailed me where there was no chance.
        I had a mind to kill him then
But couldn't make it back the way I'd come.
And even if I had climbed up
His door was never opening my way.

        When I was little, fall and cry,
My daddy said I was the one most human 'cause
I suffered most, and I believe he meant it too.
But when I got the bigger and I'd cry
He'd mock me that. So over time
I learnt his line; I mocked him back.
        And how I made the others laugh!
But I got caught.
        That's when he called me 'little goat.'
And I knew what he meant by that.
He hung his goats and slit their throats
To see they bled the better out.
I wasn't a-one to wait him that.
        Then faster than I understood my thought
He had me up and down the stairs
And landing where he stove me up to stay that way.

Sometimes I take a mind to get it right.
I study up. But there's no climbing back.
No words, because my daddy had
A preacher's words for everything,
Though I was he who made us laugh.
      But then I landed hard for that.

      Sometimes I practice what I've learnt.
I even use another voice, in point of fact."
      "I think you mean, *as case in point*," I said.
      Floyd shot me back, "I meant it like I said it;
Every object has its side from which to talk,
And some of what I just described you couldn't watch.
Meanwhile, I tell you for abiding fact
There never was a man forgive a father kicked him down.
      And all that on the day my brother bled-it-out,
And I was nowhere near for that
But just the same there was a blame on me."

      "*Well?* Well. Some tale you tell there, Floyd,
And surer for the way you cut parts out."
      "My argument exactly, Bud,
Just on a scale you've never heard before.
But rub your own small scar. See how that grows."

      "So Floyd," I said, "yours is the long truth
Tells us everything in short.
By that you beat the best there is,
The way insomnia says sleep
And just by that sees that you don't."
      "Don't fun on me," Floyd said quick back.
"I'm funnier than you, and I know more.

It's pressure gives the potent stuff.
That got me in security
And taught me the superlatives
And how the order of the other side
Is always wrong. We wouldn't have one turn
But that the other side turns opposite.
       Just try your little case alone
And see how empty that will get.
Or just you walk you down a hall or two,
Sizing stores you find along the way
Where not a lock on either side will give.
I've stood that hall; I've waited that eventual."

       And Floyd went on with stuff like that,
Till though I had another thing to say
Security had elbowed off,
Bird wings collapsing from his back
Where he was crossing for his Mercury
Still idling, its alternator giving out
So headlights up then headlights down.
       There was no June, no boy, no girl for him,
Just one door wide through which Floyd caught his hat
And worked himself behind the wheel.
Then made things turn.

Acknowledgments

I would like to thank the editors of these magazines in which some of these poems first appeared.

Blackbird: "Small Facts."

The Hopkins Review: "ad lib," "Another Christmas Tie This Year," "Bad Dog," and "Nod," sections 1 & 2.

The Kenyon Review: "Reading the Map."

Poetry: "Making Frankenstein."

The Sewanee Review: "Checks and Balances," "Thin."

Wyatt Prunty is the Ogden D. Carlton III Distinguished Professor at Sewanee: The University of the South, where he teaches poetry. The founding director of the Sewanee Writers' Conference, the Sewanee Writers' Series, and the Tennessee Williams Fellowship program, he is the author of nine books of poetry and one critical work, as well as the recipient of numerous awards and fellowships. He also serves as the chancellor of the Fellowship of Southern Writers.

John Hollander, *Blue Wine and Other Poems*

Robert Pack, *Waking to My Name: New and Selected Poems*

Philip Dacey, *The Boy under the Bed*

Wyatt Prunty, *The Times Between*

Barry Spacks, *Spacks Street, New and Selected Poems*

Gibbons Ruark, *Keeping Company*

David St. John, *Hush*

Wyatt Prunty, *What Women Know, What Men Believe*

Adrien Stoutenberg, *Land of Superior Mirages: New and Selected Poems*

John Hollander, *In Time and Place*

Charles Martin, *Steal the Bacon*

John Bricuth, *The Heisenberg Variations*

Tom Disch, *Yes, Let's: New and Selected Poems*

Wyatt Prunty, *Balance as Belief*

Tom Disch, *Dark Verses and Light*

Thomas Carper, *Fiddle Lane*

Emily Grosholz, *Eden*

X. J. Kennedy, *Dark Horses: New Poems*

Wyatt Prunty, *The Run of the House*

Robert Phillips, *Breakdown Lane*

Vicki Hearne, *The Parts of Light*

Timothy Steele, *The Color Wheel*

Josephine Jacobsen, *In the Crevice of Time: New and Collected Poems*

Thomas Carper, *From Nature*

John Burt, *Work without Hope: Poetry by John Burt*

Charles Martin, *What the Darkness Proposes: Poems*

Wyatt Prunty, *Since the Noon Mail Stopped*

William Jay Smith, *The World below the Window: Poems 1937–1997*

Wyatt Prunty, *Unarmed and Dangerous: New and Selected Poems*

Robert Phillips, *Spinach Days*

X. J. Kennedy, *The Lords of Misrule: Poems 1992–2001*

John T. Irwin, ed., *Words Brushed by Music: Twenty-Five Years of the Johns Hopkins Poetry Series*

John Bricuth, *As Long As It's Big: A Narrative Poem*

Robert Phillips, *Circumstances Beyond Our Control: Poems*

Daniel Anderson, *Drunk in Sunlight*

X. J. Kennedy, *In a Prominent Bar in Secaucus: New and Selected Poems, 1955–2007*

William Jay Smith, *Words by the Water*

Wyatt Prunty, *The Lover's Guide to Trapping*

Charles Martin, *Signs & Wonders*

Peter Filkins, *The View We're Granted*

Brian Swann, *In Late Light*

Daniel Anderson, *The Night Guard at the Wilberforce Hotel*